Expressions of Love, Poetry in Motion

by
Kimberley M. Calloway

Cork Hill Press
Indianapolis

Cork Hill Press
7520 East 88th Place, Suite 101
Indianapolis, Indiana 46256-1253
1-866-688-BOOK
www.corkhillpress.com

Trade Paperback Edition: 1-59408-267-7

Printed in the United States of America

1 3 5 7 9 10 8 6 4 2

Table of Contents

Foreword

Table of Contents
cont.

Acknowledgements

1st and foremost, I like to give honor to and praise God for the wonderful gifts He has imparted in me, and to my husband Mr. Kim Calloway who inspired me to write again.

• Special thanks to my Pastors Lawrence and Joy Hanks and all the Church members for support and encouragement.

• To my family Ronald, Kiara, Barbara, and Keisha for support and love.

• To my best friends Renea, Tracey, Angenette, Kimberly, Mary, and all of my friends at Harvard Towers Apts. and D.C.H.A. for support, encouragement, and love.

• To my Publisher/ Editor for your good eye and sharp mind, Thank You.

Foreword

Often times in analyzing works we are lost for words
to give descriptions to such a work as this, but Kimberley
has hit the nail on the head with her many authentic works.

Keeping it real and to the point, I understand why her works have so
profanely touch my heart and stirred me to write even the more.

Her cunning knack and ability to rhyme, as well as to
get her point across shows the true poet that lies within her.

Therefore I am glad to be writing this foreword, so grab hold to your heart
and watch as Kimberley wins the hearts of many avid readers everywhere.

If you have an appointment please wait until you return
to read this book, simply because, it will grab you, and before you know it, it
would have lost its opportunity to escort you to your destination.

So why read another book of poems, this is not just another book of poems,
it's the beginning of a new found Love we call "Expressions of Love"

Being an author and poet myself, I understand the true
terminology of expressive writings, so if you're
trying to say something to somebody, get the book and
let Kimberley say it for you.

Foreword 2

Just to name a few: Infatuation will lead you to A
Never Ending Love simply because your not Keeping
It Real, and you've somehow lost Reality, because
of your X, so As I Was Saying, Until We Meet Again,
Hush Don't Say A Word.

As you read this book, I hope it brings you as much joy
and laughter as it brought me, and may the pages jump out
at you and find you where you need it most for such a time as this, read on
people read on.

I like for you to know that the foreword of this book is
written by: Kimberley's husband. It's such a dying need in
men and women alike to take interest in our mates life
to show our love in what they do.

Mr. Kim Calloway
September 27, 2002

Love

God is Love, the glorious and Heavenly Father,
Who created us from above?
Love is beautiful,
Love is sweet,
Love is wonderful, and so unique.
Love is awesome,
Love is humble,
Love makes you strong, so that you won't stumble.
Love is happiness,
Love is joy,
Love shouldn't be taken lightly, because it's not a toy.
Tell me! What do you think Love means?
Well I'll tell you; it's 1st. Corinthians 13.
Love presents you without wrinkle or spot,
Because, when you Love, you Love with all of your heart.
Love is something, and the one thing you can't live without, this is
what Love is all about.
Love, Love, and more Love.

Marriage

It is written: 'He that findeth a wife findeth a good thing and obtains
favor in the Lord, you're truly a treasure to be adored.

You're my soul mate for a lifetime, two souls that intertwine,
our thoughts, our dreams, and our love combine.

You make my life complete, you're the best thing in my life,
into this relationship, you bring no strife.

What one may think, the other will feel;
this is a God given gift and this is for real.

What God has joined together no man can separate, this is a time for
joy and laughter, a time to celebrate.
Celebrate a vision created for two,
a celebration designed for both me and you.

Marriage is sacred, holy and new, marriage is a union joined by two.
Marriage is an agreement that I implore;
marriage will be around forevermore.

"ONENESS"

(Oneness the pure awesomeness of it.)

Just the sound of it alone makes me, shiver, dance and sing,
Oneness is completeness, and that's a great thing.

Two joined together, becoming as one,
is perfection designed by the "Holy One".

Oneness is whole, full, and complete,
Oneness is wholesome, special, and sweet.

Oneness is united, and never divided,
Oneness is courage, which is never discouraged.

One plus one equals = Oneness, Oneness, Oneness.

A Never-Ending Love

Love unconditional,
Love so true,
A never-ending love, is what I'll give to you.
A love that's deep as the ocean,
Love that is given completely,
A never-ending love, and this I'll give so freely.
A never-ending love, is love without limits,
and a love that's wider than the sea,
A never-ending love, is love that is given external and internally.
A never-ending love, that's given from above.
A love filled with passion, that's given with action.
A love filled with joy, can never be destroyed.
A love filled with glee, will last 'til all eternity.
A never-ending love will have no doubts,
and this is what I am talking about.

"Blessed"

For it is written: that it is more "blessed" to give than to receive,
this is an act I truly believe.

"Blessed" to be here another day,
"Blessed" is my Savior in everyway.

A "Blessing" in disguise that's what you are,
A handsome prince, and you are my star.

"Blessed" to have my family and friends in my life,
"Blessed", because I am a true friend, mother, and soon to be wife.

"Blessed" to love you with all of my heart, and this I knew from the
start, because we'll be together till death do us part.

"Blessed" am I, and this is true,
"Blessed" am I, I will call me you.
I thank God, and the angels above,
because He "Blessed" me with your love.

When I Think of You

When I think of you; I think:
Heaven must be on my side and in my favor,
This is an awesome union, and I will praise my Savior.
When I think of you, I think of unity and love,
Unleashing its fullness, deep down and high above.
A prince of valor, a man that's real,
a groom that's ready to do God's will.
When I think of you,
I think of how I'm blessed to have you in my life,
"Yes" it will be an honor to be your virtuous wife.
God broke the mold when he created you,
a man that's faithful, sensitive, and true.
When I think of you, I think I finally can exhale,
I am happy and at peace, and this you can tell.
When I think of you, I think of how well we gel,
When we look into each other's eyes, we hear wedding bells.
When I think of you, its 365 days, every week, and 24/7,
We're bound here on earth, and we're bound in Heaven.
These are some of my thoughts, when I'm thinking of you.

Togetherness

The closer I get to you; I feel brand new; like a brand new person,
which I owe all to you Lord.

You make my life complete, you turn my world around,
because I once was lost, but now I'm found.

A closer walk with thee, is what I desire, I give my heart and soul to
you; I give my entire, my entire self, and this is required, required of
me to do God's will, and this is a task, I will fulfill.

Yes I am at peace and I am free,
because I am nearer, nearer to thee.
Togetherness, closeness, nearer than near,
I have the Lord in my life, of whom shall I fear.

You're a Man

An understanding lover, friend, and fan, very secure with who you
are, because you're a man.

Dependable, but able to conquer what's set before you day to day,
you're truly blessed, you're blessed in everyway.

Strong and stable, confident in who you are, you're a real man, and
that's hard to find; yet by far.

You're so sweet and you're so tender, to you I give my all, and I totally
surrender, surrender myself, and this is true, not withholding back,
anything from you.

One thing's for sure! You're always at your best, and being who you
are, makes you different from the rest.

You're a powerful man, and you're respectful too, its truly an honor to
be in the presence of you;" Because you're my man".

Devotion

"How deep is your love"? This is my question?
Is it as deep as the ocean? Or does it run like a river?
When I tap into your mind, will I find, the answers to the
questions I long to know?

Devotion is loyalty and great love,
and this is something I yearn for, and I'm worthy of.

It's a need and a want, I'm sure you understand;
that this can only be given by, a real sincere woman or man.

Give me all of your love; give it to me,
an in return I will love you unconditionally.

"Keeping it Real"

Keeping it real, Keeping it strong,
Keeping it right, so that you do no wrong.

When you keep it real you gain trust,
So keeping it real is a must.

To keep it real you must be true and upright,
Keeping it real gives you integrity and might.

Keeping it real with loyalty and communication;
communication is eternal, and also information.

Keeping it real is playing it smart,
Keeping it real is from the heart.
Keeping it real is the deal,
and it's ideal to keep it real.

"Expressions"

A smile is a sign of pleasure or amusement.
Laughter is the act or sound of laughing.
Hugs are a form of affection by squeezing someone in your arms.
Kisses are a touch or caress of the lips.

All of these expressions are great you see, but there's nothing like these
(3) three words which are special to me.
If you haven't figured it out or if you haven't got a clue, these (3)
Three words mean: I Love You.

"Praise the Lord"

Greater is He that is in me than he that is in the world,
We're children of the King, every man, woman, boy and girl.
We're a chosen people; royal gods; for this He has spoken,
For many are called, but few are chosen.
"Praise the Lord", all ye saints, give thanks unto the Lord,
He is good all the time, a treasure to be adored.
Worship our Father that made Heaven and earth, fountains of water,
and the sea, bless the Sovereign Lord our living God: He gave His only
begotten Son who died for you and me.
Enter His gates with thanksgiving, enter His courts with praise, be
thankful, and bless His name all of your days.
So put on your garment of praise, giving thanks to the Lord always,
walk right, be obedient, and acknowledge Him in all your ways,
because when you keep all of His commandments, He will bless you
with long days.
Bless the Lord at all times, His praise shall continuously be in our
mouth I say, bow down on your knees with all supplication,
and pray, pray, pray.
The Lord is worthy; yes He's worthy, because there's something about
our Praise. "PRAISE HIM"!

Beauty

Beauty's only skin deep, beauty is passing;
beauty is within, which is everlasting.

To be beautiful on the inside and outside too,
is a divine gift, given to you.

You're simply beautiful, an attribute all of your own
with a unique attractiveness, that's yours alone.

Beauty is just a word to describe a person, place, or thing,
It's an emotion full of senses, to every human being.

There are all kinds of beauty, in this world:
animals, flowers, and even a head full of curls.

Beauty starts within, and they say that it's in the eye of the beholder,
beauty sometimes last, even when we get older.

Beauty fades with time, and this is no lie,
because beauty is a pleasure to every eye.

Faith

For it is written: that as God has dealt to each one a measure of faith, because faith cometh by hearing and hearing the word of God.

Now faith is the substance of things hoped for the evidence of things not seen, God will wipe all of your sins away, He will make you clean.

For we walk by faith not by sight, so rejoice with gladness, rejoice with delight, because everything will be all right. The Lord is Holy, this you can't ignore, For He is great; He is a treasure to be adored.

We wish, we hope, and we can achieve, with God, all things are possible, but you got to believe; believe in the Lord with all of your heart. Connect yourselves with Him, so that you can be a part; a part of His family, a child of God, He will renew your spirit and create in you a clean heart.

Without God in your life; life can be hard, because without faith it's impossible to please God.

' Faith' You Got To Have It!

Reality

Some people need a wake up call, for this isn't a fantasy,
They're living in denial, and afraid of reality.
Wake up and smell the coffee, wake up I say;
this is not a dream, act or a play.
Sometimes you let your imagination, run a little wild,
isolating yourself, as if you were a child.
Reality is too strong, for some people to bear;
some people just give up, because they just don't care.
This world we're living in, is getting closer to the end.
There is life after death, and life on the other side, so
don't get caught up in false dreams or some foolish pride.
'Wake up', 'Get up', don't live in the past,
reality's approaching, and it's approaching fast.
A daydreamer would say, it's only a dream anyway; I'm a dreamer; So
what! What's the big deal, the reality of it all, is that reality is real.

Wisdom

Fearing the Lord is the beginning of wisdom.
To be wise in your own eyes is foolish, to think you know it all is crazy,
and to do nothing with your mind is lazy.

Happy is the man who finds wisdom and gets understanding, for her
proceeds are better than silver and gold, and this is the best knowledge
ever told?

To have wisdom, knowledge, understanding, and discernment too, is
worth more than anything given to you. This is what Wisdom stands
for you see- Will, Integrity, Self-Control, Discretion, and Order that's
Manifested, within me.

Forgiveness

For unforgiveness brings on sickness, if you truly forgive,
then you can truly live.

Forgiveness is truly divine, to forgive is an act that is kind; and in your
heart you will feel fine, and it will also take a load off your mind.

Forgiveness is the key to health, wealth, and longevity, and it's the
beginning of prosperity.

To forgive somebody for anything that they may have done, is a
humbling act shown by someone?

"Visions"

I had a dream last night with a vision of you, dancing in the moonlight,
and you were all dressed in white.

You looked so pure and you danced so freely, to a special tune of
happy melodies.

The vision I had, seem so real, something that I could reach out to
touch or feel.

I envision us taking long strolls in the park, strolling all day, even until
dark.

Strolling on the beach, kicking the sand, walking together, hand and
hand.

You're a vision of loveliness; you're gentle as a dove,
You're like an iron hand in a velvet glove.

These are some of my visions of you, that I hope will come true.

With You in Mind

I think of you every night and day, the love in my heart makes me feel this way, I bow down on my knees and pray, and I thank God for you everyday.

You're always on my mind and in my heart; it was love at first sight, and it hit me like a dart.

"Lovely" is what I'll call you, you're perfect in every way, my heart, mind, soul and total being is here to stay. We will enjoy life to its fullest, and we will wine and dine, but everything I do is with you in mind.

Gospel

Go ye therefore and teach all nations, tell them about the goodness of
the Lord, and that His grace and mercy endures forever.

Tell them how He saves, delivers, and sets free, He can do all this and
more for you, and me.

Instead of backbiting or gossiping, lets preach the gospel to the world,
we have to tell every man, woman, boy, and girl.

"Tell them Now"! Don't Hesitate; "Tell them Now", before it's too late.

JOY

Unspeakable joy is something I can not hide, it can't be contained and it won't stay inside.

I am so happy, I'm like a kid with a toy, this is a great feeling, and it's a time to enjoy.

I have so much joy; I just want to shout; Hallelujah! To the Lord, I want to let it all out.

I got love deep down in my heart, that no one can destroy, I am over whelmed with glee, because you bring me "Joy".

Since, Scents, and more Sense
(The three words sound alike, but are totally different.)

"Since" I fell for you I haven't been the same, you know what's
awesome? We both have the same name.

The "Scents" that you wear smell ooh so good,
If I could wear you I would.

I have "Sense" to know that you're good for me,
You're Heaven sent, and I'm happy as can be.

"Since" you're meant for me, we will live in harmony.
Peace is what we will share, because I love you and I care.

The "Scent" of love makes my feelings flow, when you look at me you
can see my skin glow.

You set all of my "Senses" afire; you're my soul mate, the one whom I
desire.

Paradise

You're so fabulous, you're so divine,
I'm so blessed, because you're all mines.

I trust you solely with no concerns;
in your hands my heart is held firm.

I'm in paradise when I'm with you,
I got Heaven right here on earth, I thought you knew!

Paradise is Heaven in all its fullness: Peace, Harmony, Unity, and
Love, Paradise is Heaven way up in the sky above.

Rainbow

The rainbow is beautiful, for all that it's worth,
a rainbow is also a covenant between God and earth.

The colors of the rainbow are special you see,
let me tell you what they mean to me.

Red- is the Blood that cover us and wash us clean,

Purple- is for Royalty, blessings shall be seen.

Green- is for the Trees, which cleans the air and provides shade;
and this is something that God has made.

Yellow- is for the Sun that is very bright,
it was made for heat and also light.

Blue- is for the Sky and the sea,

Pink- is for cotton candy and rosary.

Orange- is a color all of its own,
it's also the name of a fruit that's known and grown.

Queen

I am your King, and you are my Queen,
and to you I give my everything.

You are the queen of my heart, the queen in my life;
you are very special to me, because you're my wife.

Some Queens are rulers of a nation, but you are the ruler of my heart,
we will be together forever, till death do we part.

You're a ruler of your own; you sit high in royalty, on your throne.
You are dear to my heart, and this I can not measure, I give my
unconditional love to you, and it's truly a pleasure.

(To My Queen)

Infatuation

My heart was beating so fast to the point I thought I was going to pass out. I'm so nervous and I'm trembling without a doubt.

You make my heart beat, you make me feel so weak; so weak in the knees, that I can't hardly stand up straight. Sometimes my words stumble, or sometimes I, I, hesitate.

I can't even think straight and I lost my train of thought, I want to say something to you, but my tongue got caught.... (Caught up.)

I have butterflies in my stomach, I have cold feet, if I could be bold enough to talk to you, it would take off some of the heat.

I think I'm in love with you: people say it's only infatuation, I want to spend my life with you, and this is my situation.

Till We Meet Again

I'm going away for a short time; I'll keep you close to my heart, but till we meet again, we'll never be apart.

Please don't be sad, and please don't cry; I can give you more than one reason why? Till we meet again, be at peace, because I care, sooner than you know it, I'll be there.

I know you'll miss me and the feelings are the same, but till we meet again, your love I do proclaim.

You will always be my lover, companion, and friend, Stay strong and hold on: Until we meet again.

"As I Was Saying"

Tried, Tested, and True; you're my greatest inspiration, and I exalt
you. For this cause: I sing songs of praise, because it's due, and this is a
celebration, I dedicate to you.

Through it all, you are faithful, and you're always there, your love is
unconditional, because you always care.

You're a friend of mine; you're gracious and merciful day to day,
You're always on time, and you're perfect in every way.

I lift your name on high, Lord; to you I am praying, I magnify your
name, and it's you I'm craving, which all comes back to...
As I was saying.

"X"

Have you ever wondered why they replaced a word
with the letter "X"?
It makes you wonder what will they do next.

Always trying to do something that they know they should not,
With a logo that says "X" marks the spot.

Like for instance: X-mas (which is Christmas) they marked out Christ:
This says a lot within itself,
Have you wondered why would they commit such stealth?

This is enough to make you want to scream and shout, and its
something to really think about.

Undeniable

You got your hooks in me, and I can not lie, you got my nose wide open, and this I can't deny.

You're "Undeniable," and to you I proclaim, my faithful and true love, and there's no need to explain.

I trust you whole-heartedly, and this you must know, that I will follow you, where ever you go.

Give me more of you, you're simply the best, you're undeniable, and this I will confess.

Zig Zag

You heard the song; you got me going in circles; you got me spinning around,
When you came into my life, my world was turned upside down.

You got me going zig zag, that I can't hardly keep my composure, I'm totally wide open, and I bare my exposure.

Since you came into my life, I haven't been the same, phenomenally speaking! Sometimes I don't even know my name.

You're a breath of fresh air, a jewel to my eye, delicate as a flower, and all I can do is sigh!
(A HUM...)

Pearls

Pearls are exquisite, and luxurious too,
it comes in all shapes, sizes, and various hues.

A creamy white gem, that's found in an oyster,
rounded to perfection, and wrapped in moisture.

People say that diamonds are a girl's best friend,
but unlike the diamond, pearls endure till the end.

Pearls and diamonds are special gems,
a treasure to those that partake of them.

You're like a pearl, well rounded in every aspect of your life;
With a hint of sensitivity, and a hint of spice.

Topped with kindness, sprinkled with class, with a touch of finesse,
you're always at your best.
You're vibrant with charisma, just to name a few,
these are just some things that describe you.

Hush! Don't say a word

"Hey listen": have you heard, please hush, and don't say a word. I want you to sit still and remain, because I have something, I want to explain:

The way you part your lips tells me what you feel for me.
The things you do tell me how much you adore me.
The way our eyes lock into place, when we see each other's face, soft kisses, soft caresses, and how we embrace.

This truly says a lot and without words, your thoughts, and gestures, you are truly heard.
Never stop telling me, never stop I say; telling me you love me, each and everyday.

You're truly special and you're sweet as can be, but as often as you can, just show me.

Ambition

Go for it, reach for the stars in everything you do, you can achieve anything, that you put your mind to.

Ambition is a drive and something to achieve, you can do all things through God, but you got to believe.

Believe in yourself, be confident, for this you must do, for knowledge is power, and it's the one thing that can not be taken from you.

"Money"

Easy come, Easy goes, money comes from trees, didn't you know?

Money makes some people do some crazy things: like rob, steal, or even kill, do you know what I mean.

The things that some people do are truly unbelievable, for the love of money, is the root of all evil.

I know we need money to pay for this and that, money is a necessity, and this is a fact.

Money is a good thing, when used in the right way, so take care of your priorities first, do you hear what I say!

You can not take it with you, when you leave this place, so be a good steward with your money, so it won't go to waste.

"Children are people too,"

What about the children, or have we forgotten about them?
They are people too; this has got to stop!
They're precious bundles of joy, little girls, and little boys.
They're a gift from God you see; He has imparted them into us, as a gift for you and me.

You have to train up a child in the way he should go, and this is something that they must know, when he is old he will never depart from it, and they can pass it on and on so that it just won't quit.

For foolishness is bound up in the heart of a child, and the rod of correction will drive it far from him, so that they don't run wild.

We have to be examples for them you see, so they will grow up to be all they're suppose to be. They are examples for us too, we just have to observe and listen to them too.

God said: Except ye are converted and become as little children we will not enter the Kingdom of Heaven. We have to have a child-like mind to love unconditionally, and forgive easily.

NAMES

What's in a name, do you want me to explain.
Its spiritual each and everyone, no two are the same, each one means a
different thing.

Like for instance, Kim means diamond in a rough,
Waiting to be captured by a special touch.

The best diamonds are found hidden deep in the soil,
To find me you have to dig deep into my soul.

With the proper care it will bring forth its luster, and its beauty.
Personally let me tell you what the name Kim means to me.

K- is for Kinsmen, a leader at heart that's what you are you see,
I- is for Intercessor, the one who would lay down his life for me.
M- is for Messenger, through your actions and your words, you have a
message and it will be heard.

Grandma

Ms. Lillian Johnson was like a grandmother to me,
A beautiful silver haired lady, just as sweet as she can be.

She loved all the children, and treated us all the same,
She knew each and everyone of us, and she knew us by name.

When we would ask? How are you doing today?
She would just smile and say:
I'm doing just fine, never had a headache in my life,
We would just sit in awe saying; that's awesome; God has blessed you,
that's all right.

In her own words I think she would say"!
I'm going on home now, to meet my Father in Heaven for He is great, I
know you're sad and mourning, but I want you to celebrate.
Celebrate my home going, where there's nothing but singing, shouting,
and praising the Lord all day,
When you think of me, think of me in this way.

Always with happiness, laughter, and joy in your heart,
I'm living on in Heaven and in your memories, so we'll never be apart.
"(This is dedicated to a special lady in my life.)"

"Cake"

Chocolate, Vanilla, 'ooooh' lick-a-de split,
So many flavors and kinds to choose from, just take your pick.

A delight to the mouths that partake of her: and such a wonderful
treat, it's so delicious, tasty, and sweet.
Cake, that's what I'll call you, because all these things describe you.

You are sugar and spice and every thing nice, that's what you are
made of.

I'll give you my last bite, because it's totally all right.
Truly delectable for this is true, 'Cake', my favorite treat from me to
you.

Two peas in a pod

We're so much alike, and I can't explain, we have so much in common, we're exactly the same.

This is a quality, I'm learning to like, you know what's funny, we even look alike.

We're one in the same, me and you; this can take some getting use to.

At first I thought, this was really odd, Hey! 'We're 'Twins, 'Two peas that were in one pod.   Literally! Ha Ha!

FEAR

LOOK-A-HERE, LOOK-A-HERE, Let me hip you to the deal; fear is nothing but False Evidence Acting Real.

For God has not given us the spirit of fear, but of power, love, and a sound mind, so you can be peaceful and not confined.

There is no fear in love, but perfect love casts out all fear, because fear involves torment. So get over your fears, cast them out, trust in the Lord, and never doubt.

Rest Assure

I say rest, gently rest; and don't you worry,
Lay your head on my shoulder, take your time, and don't be in a
hurry.

You can rest assure that everything will be all right, be strong hold on
don't give up, hold tight.

Cast all of your cares on the Lord, and totally rest, be happy, and at
peace and always at your best.

Patience is a task, you must endure, I want you to relax and rest
assure.

The Air that you Breathe

"Why do some people always say;" I have to see it to believe it.
Well just sit and let me tell you about it.

The air that you breathe can not be seen, but you know that it's there,
Some people take it for granted, because they just don't care.

How can they do this, when they know it isn't the right thing to do, we
even think we made ourselves, just to name a few?

The air that you breathe is precious for you and me, it's so precious
that even a blind man can see. Its value is worth more than silver and
gold, and it's what God breathed into man, that he became a living
soul.

"When You Get Right Down To It"

Life can be full of chances from day to day, so don't get caught up in
your circumstances, when trials and tribulations come your way.

Get up and shake it off, don't go out on the border, hang in their, life
goes on, just get yourselves in order.

It's true that sometimes things tend to get a little rough, but it's time to
say to yourself I ain't taking no more stuff, because enough is enough.

We have to stand firm in this day and time, trust in the Lord and keep
the faith, so that you won't lose your mind.

It's time to get our act together and get more education, because when
you get right down to it, we all need to stay focused, in every situation.

"The Finer Things in Life"

Taking trips to the islands, taking long walks,
going to the movies, and to amusement parks.

Lying out on the beach, getting a tan,
lying next to your lady, or your man.

Watching all types of sports, in person or on TV,
snuggled up to your baby and your family.

Going on boat rides, and horseback riding too,
there's just all types of fun, for both me and you.

Playing board games, going to the mall,
lying around just kicking it, and having a ball.

Wining and dining, with family, friends, husband, or wife,
these are just some of the finer things in life.

"The Best is Yet to Come"

Blessed are we as a people yes indeed, the Lord helps the poor, heavy-laden, and broken that's really in need.

Jesus is the way, the truth, and the light, He is perfect and glorious, and He will help you walk right.

He walked amongst us, we comprehended it not, and we were so into ourselves, that we completely forgot; all of the mighty works, that He has done, He did this and more for everyone.

He came down the first time to die for us, and He passed the test, but when things go wrong in our lives, we call on Jesus to get us out of our mess.

His grace and mercy has brought us thus far and then some, but His Second Coming will be the best that is yet to come.

"It's You That I Need"

So high spirited, sweet and gentle, always giving of yourself, you're very sentimental.

Like a breath of fresh air, you blew into my life, making me whole and complete; you bring no strife.

I can't help but notice that I am blessed, I pray that everyone will find someone like you, with much success.

To my heart you have the lock and the key, it's you that I need, because you complete me.

"Take a Little Time"

How are you doing? Fine I would hope, take a little time for yourself, so you can cope, with all of the things going on around you in everyday life, so much misery, so much strife.

Take a little time, to bow down and pray, God is listening, to every word you say.

No need to worry, no need to fear, everything will be alright, because God is near.

Just keep in mind, that in your heart you'll find, a love so divine, so please don't sit around and pout, because God will work it all out, beyond the shadow of a doubt.

I'm sure things will be alright, and things will work out just fine, but all you have to do is, just take a little time.

"Let Me Take You There"

My heart is pounding, and this I can not hide, I have a deep love for
you, that I just can't keep inside.

Come step into my world, its not a world of make believe, let me take
you there, so you can receive.

A love that's so wide open, and not hidden under cover, a love that is
special, and unlike no other.

So open up your heart, so we can share, joy and happiness together,
because I care. I will fill your heart, with laughter and glee, we will
always be together, and you can depend on me.

Trust in me, and I will give you my heart, together we'll be, and never
grow apart.
Give me a chance, now that you're aware, the two of us together, as a
pair, but all I want you to do is; Let me take you there.

"Heaven"

A place where you can be carefree, and treated kind, a place where
there are no worries, where you can have a peace of mind.

A place where we often hope and dream of, a place way up in the sky,
that's full of joy and love.

A place with dancing, happiness, and laughter, a place not here on
earth, but in the here after.

Heaven is the place where you definitely want to be, with a peace that
surpasses all understanding.

"New Beginnings"

I once was lost going in circles, I was going no where, I was about to
give up, because I thought that no one seem to care, but then I met
you, old faithful and true, I give my heart and I give my soul to you.

I wore a frown, but now I wear a smile, you came into my life and
turned it around.
I'm very happy and I am free, because now I have a new identity.
Just when you think, you're a lost cause, Jesus shows up, and shows
you whose boss.

I can't thank Him enough, but I will thank Him anyway, because He
opened up my eyes, to see a new day.
Now I have a new beginning, it's a brand new day; I'm starting all over
now, in a fresh new way. I thank the Lord and to Him I will pray,
praising His name each and everyday.

"People Pleasers"

You can't please people all of the time; this is something you have to
keep in mind.

Why do we have a need to please other's so; you have a mind of your
own; you know?

You don't have to get peoples approval or opinions too; all you have to
do is, be confident within you.

People will take you for granted, because you're so kind, honesty and
truthfulness is so hard to find.

Trying to please people, and loosing your identity, because you're so
wrapped up in what they think or see.

People will tell you anything, to keep you in the blind; they will run
you ragged if you let them, with your state of mind.

Look in the mirror! What do you see? A vision of "yourself" with such
clarity.

Please do yourselves a favor, before you blink, stop worrying about
what other people think.

"Someone Cares"

Hey! Stop walking around with a non-chalant attitude, be thankful for what you've got, and show a little gratitude.

Carrying that burden around, is bad for your health, but first it starts with you caring about yourself.

Your family and friends care for you too, but there is a greater "One" who cares about you.

His name is Jesus, and He knows what you're going through, even when you don't know what to do.

Just keep it in your heart, an always be aware, and always remember that someone cares.

"King"

I am your queen, and you are my king, and to you I give my everything.

You are the king in my life, the king of my heart, we will be together, till death do us part.

Some kings are rulers of a nation, but you're the head of my life, I am your queen, and I am your wife.

You're a ruler of your own, you sit high on your throne, you're dear to my heart, this I can not measure, I give my unconditional love to you, and it's truly a pleasure.

(To my King)

"Kindness"

You take everything in with a smile, and you're always striving to be your best, you never worry or complain, very confident within yourself.

You're tender at heart, warm and sensitive, you display such kindness that you so freely give.

This is something that can change people's lives in a special way, because kindness is an act that's rarely shown in this world today.

I'm so glad that there's still a few of you left in this day and time, please stay as you are, and everything will work out just fine.

How Long?

Patiently waiting, you're always on my mind, can't wait until we be together, everything will be just fine.

I've waited all of my life to be with you, to finally have you in my life, would be a dream come true.

I know the saying goes, be anxious for nothing, but I'm so excited that I just want to sing.

I want to be your love of a lifetime, because with you is where I belong, I just have one question to ask? How long?

Carefree

Don't worry about tomorrow, because tomorrow can take care of itself, being stressed out, or worrying about everything, is bad for your health.

Don't let the cares of this world burden you down, stop being depressed, or just sitting around.

Don't get caught up in all of your emotions, just relax, and take it easy, and stop all of the commotion.

Do think on these things, peace, love, and hope, do your best and take it easy, so that you can cope.

Do yourself a favor, and be happy for a change, you deserve the better and the best of everything.

This is something that can pertain to you or me; all you simply have to do is, be carefree.

"Inspiration"

I was a hopeless fool, I had no direction, you brought meaning in my life, with reproof and correction.

You inspired me to go on, even when I didn't want to, you're truly an angel from Heaven, and I'm glad you helped me, because it gave me a new view.

You lift me up, to places I've never known, it's because of you, my self-esteem has grown.

I thank you Lord for what you have done; and this is a special occasion; I have a new meaning of life now, because you're my inspiration.

Forever Mine

You are my soul mate, you are my friend, and we'll always be together through thick and thin.

We'll be together through the good times, and the bad times too, together forever, just us two.

A lover of a lifetime, and close companion too, I am happy to spend the rest of my life with you.

Long life and prosperity is what we'll share, together forever what a perfect pair.

My heart with your heart are one combine, I sure am glad that you are forever mine.

Busy Body

You're so busy; busy as you can be; you're just a busy body, giving yourself to anybody.

Always flaunting yourself around, and giving into temptation, being conspicuous all the time, leaving nothing to the imagination.

I know sometimes in our lives, we all make mistakes, but doing it just for the heck of it, I just can't relate.

I don't know what's going on, in people's mind today, they need direction and stability, so that they won't go astray.

I know sometimes self-esteem, plays a part in this, and its over-rated, early on in our lives, we should have been validated.

Self-control is what you need, without a doubt, stop being a busy body, before you become all worn out.

There's nothing wrong with being celibate, or being a virgin, save what God gave to you, for your future wife or husband.

Please Stop! Stop what you're doing as soon as you can, stop running around from woman to woman or from man to man.

Don't Let it Get You Down

You may be going through some changes or circumstances, and have a lot on your mind; situations do tend to turn around, just in the nick of time.
Trials or troubles won't be here everyday, even though sometimes it seem like it won't go away, don't look at your circumstances or where they came from, its just a minor set back that you soon will overcome.

Sometimes we get caught in between a rock and a hard place, being depressed won't help the situation, or having a sad look on your face. You hide your true feelings and emotions, just to keep from breaking down, don't feel sorry for your self, take it all in with a smile, because it will get better after while.

Why do people tend to question your maturity, when all you needed was just a little security.
Hold your head up, don't give up, stop all that moping around, be strong, keep the faith, and don't let it get you down.

JEALOUSY

You can't stand to see another advance, because you just can't cope,
what makes you happy, is to see others in the same boat.

Always turning your nose up and looking down on people is really low;
always complaining or being puffed up is not the way to go.

Stop blaming people for what they have, and don't give into hating,
keep the green-eyed monster under wraps, and start anticipating.

Jealousy is an evil thing, that no one should harbor within, being
envious isn't good either, it's just jealousy's twin.

Now after reading this, I hope you've changed your mind, instead of
being jealous; why don't you try being kind.

Friends for Life

Sometimes true friends are hard to find, but I'm glad that you are a true friend of mine.

You're very patient with me, and you're never in a hurry, you speak words of comfort to me, so that I never worry.

You speak the truth sometimes, and I have a fit, constructive criticism is good for me, and this I can admit.

You're my friend when I'm up, my friend when I'm going through, my friend always, even when I doubted you.

You always look at the positive side of everything, when I'm being negative; you're a blessing in disguise, that makes me want to live.

We're friends for life; you and I, we'll be friends forever, until the day we die. A friend will stick closer than a brother, and this is true, you're like no other, and I cherish you.

Happy Baby

She's so bubbly, cheerful, and bright; she's so precious and beautiful
in our sight.

She's always spreading her happiness around, and it's so contagious
you can't help but smile.

Freely giving of herself, and with a sincere heart, gentle, tender, and
very smart.

Bold and confident within herself, because she's a lady, nothing can
really get her down, because she's a happy baby.

Express Yourself

It's okay to have your own belief and to have your own voice, you have
that right, and the freedom of choice.

People express themselves in many different ways; we all have our own
unique quality and unique traits.

To be who you are, or what you become, is all in your hands, it's just
an impression made by one without any demands.
Just go for what you know and apply yourself to everything that you
do, because when it's all said and done its really left up to you.

"Unforgettable"

Sweet thoughts and memories of you, that were left behind, all of them
seem to linger in my mind.

Joking and playing around, having a laugh or two, having a good time
with family and friends, enjoying our rendezvous.

So mature and wise, you're unlike no other, very kind and
understanding, you would go out of your way for another.

You have a heart of gold and you're truly incredible, how can anyone
forget someone like you, because you're truly unforgettable.

Equal

Don't be high-minded; turning your nose up at everyone that you think is beneath you, if you should fall, whose there to pick up after you.

Don't look down on a man unless your picking him up, having a snobbish attitude is all messed up.

Why do you act the way that you do, didn't you know we're all equal? We may look different, but we're one in the same, don't be conceited or proud, we all have the same aim.

There's a saying that all men are created equal, and no one is better than the other, we all are connected, in one way or another.

"Roses"

Roses are Red,

Roses are Pink,

Roses are a symbol of love; that creates a link, a link between people for the sake of love, two hearts combine, becoming one thought, one mind.

Roses are a symbol of friendship, Roses are given in delicate situations, and Roses are also given on special occasions.

Roses come in a variety of colors, for your choice of fun; Roses are beautiful flowers, enjoyed by everyone.

"Submission"

Stop being stubborn and disobedient; ready to give up and quit, try
the Lords way, give in, and submit.

By becoming humble, you won't stumble, do what's right, so that your
life won't crumble.

Submit yourselves to every ordinance of man for the Lords sake: for
this is the will of God; do this as unto Him, for it isn't very hard.

Confess all of your short comings to the Lord, so that you can be
blessed, confess them now, so that you can get out of your mess.

By doing this, you put to silence the ignorance of foolish men, doing it
as unto the Lord; you don't mind doing it over and over again.

When you bring forth your petition with obedience and submission,
God will help you out of your present condition,
But all you have to do is be submissive.

"The Center of my Joy"

I put you first and foremost as the Head of my life, You are My
Bridegroom, and I am your husband or wife.

Without you in my life, my life will be a wreck that I can not trust; I
can't go back to my old life now, because it will be hard for me to
adjust.

I've come a long way, and there's no turning back: no way no how; I
have a brand new outlook on life now.
To Him I pray for waking me up everyday and in Him I will stay.
Everything that I do it revolves around you; "Jesus" is the love of my
life, and the center of my joy.

About the Author

Mrs. Kimberley M. Calloway was born and raised in Washington, DC. At the age of 15 she first began to write poetry as a means of expressing and understanding her feelings. She graduated from Eastern High School and Chamberlain Career Center where she majored in English and Cosmetology and became a licensed Beautician. She also attended NBS Law Enforcement Academy and majored in Security. She attended From the Heart Ministries Pastored by Rev. John Cherry. Now she is an ordained Evangelist of the Tribe of Juda Worship Center Pastored by Pastors Lawrence and Joy Hanks.

This book is full of poetry that ministers to your mind and soul.

I'm writing this book to stir up your gifts so that you can open up your heart and mind to receive and enjoy my heart felt messages presented to you in my book.

Printed in the United States
17595LVS00007B/1-102